The Leadership Bus

How to be a Truly Effective and Successful Leader

by
Ted Corcoran

www.theleadershipbus.com

authorHOUSE®

AuthorHouse™ UK Ltd.
500 Avebury Boulevard
Central Milton Keynes, MK9 2BE
www.authorhouse.co.uk
Phone: 08001974150

First published by AuthorHouse 7/28/2008

ISBN: 978-1-4389-0123-7 (sc)

Printed in the United States of America
Bloomington, Indiana

This book is printed on acid-free paper.

Table of Contents

Understanding Leadership

What is leadership?

Leaders come in all shapes and sizes, young and old, men and women. You can find them anywhere, for example, in politics, business, church, community and sport: in fact, you will find leaders everywhere there is a requirement for people to work together to achieve something. They can be paid or unpaid, full time or part time, CEOs or simply volunteers. They can be extremely well known or, as many great leaders are, totally anonymous to those outside their immediate circle. What they all have is the ability to harness the energy of those around them to achieve their goals. They know that you manage things, but you lead people.

It is claimed that there are over 15,000 books written about leadership, yet, for many people, it remains one of the hardest subjects to understand and particularly to put into practice. Many eminent people have written on the subject and there are nearly as many definitions as there are books written about it. So let's have a look at some of these definitions and see can we establish any common themes.

The first is by Warren Bennis, Professor of Business Administration, University of Southern California, who has extensively studied and written about leadership for many decades.

"Leadership is the capacity to translate vision into reality."

Warren Bennis

This definition is simple to understand. Every good/ great leader has a vision of some sort – in other words he/she sees in their minds eye some desired state in the future and then motivates his/her team to work towards achieving this. In Warren Bennis's words they succeed, through their people, in making the vision become real or achieved. Otherwise known as a successful outcome.

"Leadership is action, not position."
Donald H. McGannon

These five words say an awful lot. There is no use having a grand vision if there is no action to achieve it. There is absolutely no benefit in dreaming great dreams and just sitting back waiting for them to happen all by themselves. There is an even more important truth in this definition. Just because a person occupies a leadership position doesn't necessarily make that person a leader. Many of us have experienced the situation, where a person, totally unsuited to that role, is our leader and, just because they have the title, they think (or do they even do that!) that that's all that is necessary. Those unfortunate to work for these "leaders" are left to work out for themselves their own priorities and how successful they are in achieving them. Are these people happy at their work, contented that they are playing their part in the success of whatever they are involved in, and motivated to work their socks off for their "leader"? Well, what do you think? Would you? Or, more personally, have you done so, if you were ever in that unfortunate position?

"Leadership is the special quality which enables people to stand up and pull the rest of us over the horizon."

James L. Fisher

While the first two definitions expressed leadership from the point of view of the leaders, this one by James Fisher looks at it from the vantage point of the followers. This again is all about having a vision and articulating it in such a way that the followers feel compelled to, in fact eagerly want to, go where the leader desires. By the use of the phrase "over the horizon", however, Fisher infers that this desired place, while clearly visible to the leader, remains out of sight of the followers, until the leader shows them what is possible. Fisher describes leadership as a "special quality" indicating it's part of the personal makeup of the leader and somewhat rare.

"Leaders don't force people to follow——they invite them on a journey."

Charles S. Lauer

Lauer articulates the same idea. Leaders create this exciting picture of the future which their followers buy in to and eagerly work towards.

"Leadership: the art of getting someone else to do something you want done, because he wants to do it."

Dwight D. Eisenhower

When former President Eisenhower said this it was the norm for formal leaders to be men only. Things have changed a lot since and now women leaders can be found in every walk of life. And that's only as it should be. Again, what he is saying is that the secret of leadership is creating a desire in the "someone else" to do whatever is required.

So what was the common theme running through these definitions? They can be summarized as follows:

- The leader must have a vision – a clear picture of a desired future state

- The leader must articulate this in a fashion which arouses excitement and commitment among the   followers to such an extent that they will do everything possible to help achieve it

- The leader must be active in the role, not passive, never relying on the leadership position occupied, but on the personal leadership skills he/she possesses

Why is Leadership important

A good question. Many of us, at one time or another, have worked for someone whom we loved working for. We looked forward to being at work every day and our time there just flew by. Unfortunately, we have also had the very opposite experience, where we did not look forward very much to being at work. Neither did we feel connected to our leader (boss), nor regrettably to the work we were required to do. Can you imagine if everyone at a business or organization felt like this? The cumulative effect would be nothing short of disastrous. If, in addition, there was no vision at the highest levels, the business or organization could not survive very long. Warren Bennis, as usual, puts it very well in the following few words.

"A business short of capital can borrow money and one with poor location can move, but a business short on leadership has little chance of survival."

Warren Bennis

Change is inevitable in every walk of life and this, naturally, includes organizations of every shape and size. The organization that doesn't change with the changing circumstances around it is doomed to failure sooner or later. To survive and prosper every organization needs leaders and leadership – leaders who can formulate and articulate a vision that ensures its continuing prosperity and future success. And the people who deliver this prosperity and success? Everybody who works for the organization, of course, from the newest recruit to the Managing Director or Chief Executive Officer, or whoever occupies the top position. And success, or otherwise, depends largely on the conditions created by the boss or bosses, because every organization of any size has several layers of management, from front line managers to the very top. Daniel Goleman has done a lot of research on how a company's climate affects business performance and this is what he says:

"How people feel about working at a company (climate) can account for 20 to 30 per cent of business performance. If climate drives business results, what drives climate? Roughly 50 to 70 per cent of how employees perceive their organisation's climate can be traced to the actions of one person: the leader. More than anyone else, the boss creates the conditions that directly determine people's ability to work well."

Daniel Goleman, Harvard University

Who are the Leaders in any Organisation

It's a strange thing but our natural tendency is to regard our immediate boss as our leader, which he/she is, of course, never considering that, for the people who report to us, they see us as their leaders. We naturally look up for leadership and, oftentimes, forget that other people are looking at us for that very same thing. In fact, when I have asked attendees at training seminars how many of them are leaders, very few answer in the affirmative. Yet all these were managers of some level or another.

"There are many leaders, not just one. Leadership is distributed. It resides not solely in the individual at the top, but in every person at every level who, in one way or another, acts as a leader to a group of followers — wherever in the organisation that person is, whether shop steward, team head or CEO."

Daniel Goleman, Harvard University

Leadership advice worth many billions!

"I have an absolute belief that success depends upon maintaining a happy workforce. If you talk to people anywhere in the world they want four things from work:
- A job that is interesting to do

- A chance to get on in life

- To be treated with respect

- A boss who is some help and not their biggest problem

If that's all you do each day, try to give them these things, and they will follow you anywhere."

Sir Terry Leahy CEO Tesco (a leading
supermarket chain in the UK)

Sir Terry Leahy was born and grew up in very humble circumstances in Liverpool, England. He joined Tesco straight after graduating from the University of Manchester Institute of Science and Technology (UMIST) in 1979. He entered the supermarket chain as a marketing executive, was appointed to Tesco's board of directors in 1992, and by the time he was 40 he had worked his way up to become chief executive in 1997. He was chosen as Britain's "Business Leader of the Year" in 2003 and the Fortune European Businessman of the year for 2003. In 2005 he was selected as Britain's most admired business leader by *Management Today*.

His simple homespun advice has helped make Tesco the leading supermarket chain in the U.K. with profits for

2005 of about £2 billion. None of his advice is difficult to put into practice, yet how rarely do we see it done. I particularly like the reference to the boss who is some help and not the biggest problem. Could that ever apply to any of us?

The Five Practices of Exemplary Leadership

The Five Practices of Exemplary Leadership® (Jim Kouzes and Barry Posner, "The Leadership Challenge") resulted from intensive research to determine the leadership competencies that are essential in getting extraordinary things done in organizations. To conduct the research, Kouzes and Posner collected thousands of experiences people recalled, when asked to think of a peak leadership experience. This is what they found these exemplary leaders do.

They:
- Challenge the process

- Inspire a shared vision

- Enable others to act

- Walk the talk / Model the way

- Encourage the heart

Challenge the process
Exemplary leaders search for ways to change/improve their organisations. They are never satisfied with the status

quo, so they never sit back and say to themselves we are as good as we can be.

Inspire a shared vision
We have already seen that successful leaders always have a vision – a clear picture of a desired future state which they are passionate about and are able to transfer this passion to their followers. If it's not shared, then it has very little chance of happening.

Enable others to act
Leaders build teams that are both confident and capable. They work tirelessly to strengthen the knowledge and all round capacity of team members. By actively involving others around them, they give people a sense of ownership which leads to higher performance. They are excellent at aligning the various functions within their organization, company, or even team, towards common goals. They make timely decisions and do not procrastinate. No member of their team is ever unsure what they are expected to do next.

Walk the talk / Model the way
Leaders lead by example. They do what they say they will do. They keep their promises even when it is difficult for them to do so. They have integrity, a characteristic of leaders, which in several studies has been shown, by a long way, to be the most highly valued of all.

Encourage the heart
In every venture there will be times when heads will drop, the ultimate goal seems far away, and spirits get lower and lower. These are the times when great leaders remain

optimistic and speak in positive terms about the successes which are just around the corner. Even in ordinary times, special leaders go out of their way to recognize significant contributions of their people, thus satisfying a deep human need to be appreciated.

A definition of management

"The art of getting things done through people."
Frederick W. Taylor

An American engineer, Frederick Winslow Taylor (1856 – 1915), sought to improve industrial efficiency. Sometimes called "The Father of Scientific Management", Taylor made his name formulating and implementing new work methods for getting an increased output from fewer workers. In his time, new workers relied on copying their colleague's way of doing things, or on what was called "rule of thumb". There never was a question in those days of involving workers in any decisions about better or faster ways of doing things – they just provided the necessary muscle. They carried out orders with no attempt being made by management to make them feel part of a team, or show them what success looked like. They were never made feel any part, not to mind an important part, of the company or organization. And this is what Taylor's definition exactly conveys! Management is the art of getting things done through people, whether they like it or not. And people do not like working, nor do they produce their best, in conditions such as these. Usually, they do not stick around too long either. Would you?

In times past, however, people didn't have much choice. Taylor once described the good worker as someone whose job was to do "just what he is told to do, and no back talk. When the foreman tells you to walk, you walk; when he tells you to sit down, you sit down". A supervisor from this old school, who once worked for me, had a simple rule for getting by, 'Just follow the last order'. And this he faithfully did, even though many times he knew there was a better way, but never had the desire or motivation to articulate it.

The difference between management and leadership

"Great leaders unleash the collective talent and passion of people toward the right goal. Both management and leadership is vital and either one without the other is insufficient."

Dr. Stephen Covey, "On Management and Leadership"

The terms "management" and "leadership" are often spoken about as if they are the same thing. But, in fact, they are as different as chalk and cheese! However, they are both vital activities of every successful organisation. So, what are some of the things that need to be managed? The list is endless, but certainly covers areas like processes, systems, and physical assets. Leadership, on the other hand, is all about people. You manage things, but you lead people. Management could be considered the "what" you do, while leadership is the "how" you do it. If management is a process, then leadership is the oil that lubricates it.

Dr Covey, himself, a household name in the world of leadership, author of the bestselling book "The 7 Habits of Highly Effective People", freely admits, that early on in his career, while he was touring the world lecturing on leadership, his business back in Utah suffered from a lack of management. It was only when he put the necessary systems and processes in place to manage his business that it thrived; hence this quote.

The difference between managing and doing

As a manager do you spend enough of your time on management/leadership type activities? Managers, especially newly promoted managers, find they are still deeply involved in "doing" activities, giving some of following reasons for doing so: "I can do the work better than my staff can", "We would never get the work done if I didn't help", "I feel a lot less guilty when I help out" And so on and so on.

You are managing when you are planning, organizing, implementing, controlling/monitoring and reviewing. You are not managing when you are doing your staff's work for them. But if you have come to a "managing" role from a "doing" role, as very many people do, then you will find it very difficult to let your previous role go as it were. However, it is absolutely necessary to do so if you are to be successful in your new role.

Are you a Lone Ranger manager?

Managers, who jump in to help at every opportunity, I call Lone Ranger managers. The Lone Ranger, if you recall (and if you can't, it means you're a lot younger than I am!), was a famous movie character back in the 50's and 60's. Together with his loyal helper, Tonto, they responded to crises in various western U.S. towns. They rode in, the masked Lone Ranger on his beautiful white stallion, took control of the situation, sorted out the baddies to the satisfaction of the townspeople, and then left town as quickly as they arrived in a flurry of dust and to the sound of galloping hooves. However, there was no guarantee that, if the problem reoccurred, the Lone Ranger would be at hand to solve it. And this is exactly what happens when you, as the manager, do the staff's work for them, rather than showing them what to do, then allowing them to do it and to learn from the experience. If you do it for them, then they are not learning and if the problem reoccurs it will again be left to you to solve. Cue the harassed manager!

Understanding yourself
as a leader

What powers have you?

"Nearly all men can stand adversity, but if you want to test a man's character, give him power."

Abraham Lincoln

"Power tends to corrupt and absolute power corrupts absolutely."

Lord Acton 1887

As a leader, what powers have you? Have you:

- Legitimate power?

- Reward power?

- Coercive power?

- Referent power?

- Expert power?

If you have all of these, then count yourself lucky!

Legitimate Power:

The difference between a boss and a leader: a boss says, 'Go!' - a leader says, 'Let's go!'

E.M. Kelly, "Growing Disciples", 1995

The leader has the right to request or order people to do something. If you work for a boss of any type, then he/she possesses legitimate power. If people work under your control, then you, too, possess legitimate power. Just because you possess it does not mean you go around shouting instructions at everyone and expecting them to obey. That might be the way of some managers, but it's certainly not how leaders behave. How do you, yourself, prefer to be asked to do something? Ordered or requested? I thought so. And I'll bet your people would feel the same.

Coercive Power:

The leader can discipline people for non adherence to rules and regulations or unacceptable behaviour. He/she can warn, suspend, or even dismiss erring employees. It's, sadly, a fact of life that people will not always behave in an acceptable manner and this needs to be dealt with appropriately; otherwise the morale of the remaining staff will suffer. And there is an acceptable way of implementing disciplinary action. Leaders do it with sensitivity and courtesy, always conscious of the feelings of the other party.

Reward Power:

The leader controls the rewards e.g. pay increases, promotions etc. This is the enjoyable side of leadership. But, having the authority to reward brings its own downsides. Not everyone will be happy with either the size or timing of pay increases, and not everyone who applies for promotion will be successful.

Expert Power:

The leader has special knowledge or expertise. There are specialists in every organisation, but not every one of them occupies a formal leadership position. These are known as informal leaders and they, very often, purely because of their expertise, possess great power. Better have them on your side than not.

Referent Power:

People do things because they admire the leader, want to be like the leader and want to receive the leader's approval

> "Being powerful is like being a lady; if you have to tell people you are you aren't."
>
> Margaret Thatcher

Your leadership style

Every leader has a predominant style. Studies have been carried out by very famous academics over many years into the personal style of leaders, while there are also numerous books written on the subject. Each study or book describes its findings differently and often in language that non academic people find difficult to understand. Here are my descriptions of the various styles in everyday language.

- Visionary

- Mentor/Coach

- Best friend

- Consensus Seeker

- Driven

- Dictator

Here is a brief description of each.

Visionary style leadership:

"Ten years from now, we want magazines to write about GE as a place where people have the freedom to be creative, a place that brings out the best in everybody, an open fair place where people have a sense that what they do matters, and where that sense of accomplishment is rewarded in both the pocketbook and the soul. That will be our report card."

Jack Welsh, CEO General Electric

This style has a very positive impact on the climate of a company or organization (climate simply means how people feel about their company or organization). It is appropriate when a new vision or clear direction is needed. Always bear in mind, however, that vision without action achieves little.

Mentor/Coach:

This style leader encourages and guides team members to a higher standard of performance. You communicate your belief in a person's potential and create an expectation that they can do even better. It has a very positive effect on climate. But, beware, in case you fall into the trap of micromanaging.

> "A true leader is not the one with the most followers, but one who creates the most leaders."
>
> Neale Donald Walsch

Best friend:

This style leader likes to get on with everyone and is very empathic with their emotional needs. It has, as you might imagine, a very positive impact on climate. The downside is that these leaders find it very difficult to offer corrective feedback, in case this adversely affects their personal relationship with the employee.

Consensus Seeker:

This leadership style is noted for its ability to listen to people's ideas and opinions before making a decision. People feel involved and that they matter. Taken too far, people lose faith in the leader's ability to make decisions and, of course, it's the ideal hiding place for the perennial procrastinator.

Driven:

The leader with this style wants everything done yesterday. This is fine for a short term urgent project but does not work in the long term. Mostly, it's highly negative on climate as these highly driven leaders are so focused on their goals they forget or ignore the very people who are making it happen for them. People under this style of leadership enjoy it for a while, but then slowly get burned out, may get frequent illnesses and, often, finally quit.

Dictator:

Many of us have worked one time or another for dictator style leaders who control everything and make all decisions. With this type of leader "it's my way or the highway". Did you enjoy the experience? I most certainly didn't. But, in a major crisis, this is the style that achieves the most. Rudy Giuliani, post 9/11, didn't hang around being nice to people and holding endless meetings. No, he quickly made one decision after another and got New York back on its feet in no time. But, used constantly in ordinary situations, it has a highly negative effect on climate.

One of these styles may be your preferred style. I find that the predominant styles of the people who attend my seminars are Mentor/Coach, Best Friend, and Consensus Seeker - very few Visionary, Driven, or Dictator styles. Maybe they just didn't want to admit it. The thing to remember, however, is that all these styles have a place in a leader's armory. As we know from experience, different people and situations require different approaches. The secret is for the leader to judge which style is appropriate when dealing with any particular situation. Recognise which style(s) needs working on in your case and add it to your skill set.

The personal makeup of great leaders

- They have high levels of emotional intelligence

- They possess certain essential qualities

- They have special personal characteristics

Emotional Intelligence

"Refers to the capacity for recognising our own feelings and those of others, for motivating ourselves, and for managing emotions well in ourselves and in our relationships."

Daniel Goleman, "Working with Emotional Intelligence"

Daniel Goleman's bestseller "Working with Emotional Intelligence" added a new term to our daily vocabulary and fundamentally changed the way we perceive personal excellence. His research revealed that the top performers in every field from entry level to senior executive positions are distinguished from the rest by their levels of emotional intelligence. People with high EI are blessed with high levels of self awareness, self confidence, and self control, commitment and integrity. They have the ability to communicate well and by so doing are able to influence people and situations. Because they like to initiate, they can readily accept change. Goleman says that these star performers stand out, not only by personal achievement, but by their capacity to work well on teams and with people. They maximise every group's productivity. According to Goleman, EI accounts for as much as 70% of individual performance, whereas cognitive ability and technical know how account for only 30%.

They are good at managing relationships with others through among other things:

Empathy
- Understanding others

- Giving positive feedback

Social Skills
- Team capabilities

- Communication

A team can everything going for it – the brightest and most qualified people, access to resources, a clear mission – but still fail because it lacks group Emotional Intelligence

Harvard Business Review

Essential qualities of leaders

Here is a list of 12 qualities of leaders. Please rank them from 1 to 12 in the order you consider them essential. Place what you consider the most essential quality at #1 and so on down to #12.

1. Dedicated

2. Expert

3. Model

4. Courageous

5. Motivator

6. Other

7. Visionary

8. Decision maker

9. People Focused

10. Communicator

11. Integrity

12. Caring

Don't look until you have completed the exercise but you will find the results on the next page.

The most essential quality of leaders is...

Integrity

Integrity is by far the most essential quality of a leader according to a survey of 54,000 people published in Stephen Covey's book, The 8th Habit, Free Press, New York, 2004, in which they were asked to rank the above qualities in order of importance. In fact, integrity received double the votes of the next quality. Are you surprised? Have you ever worked for a boss without integrity? Was it a pleasant experience? In a separate survey conducted by Jim Kouzes, joint author of "The Leadership Challenge", trust received the highest vote. Trust and integrity go hand in hand so there is no contradiction. Integrity is what great leaders possess; accordingly, their people trust them.

Integrity Is Your Best Friend

Having integrity enables you to:

- Walk the talk

- Keep your word

- Keep your priorities right

- Stay the right course even when the wrong course is easier

- Keep going when others criticize you unfairly

> "Trust and confidence in the top leadership is the single most reliable predictor of employee satisfaction in an organisation"
>
> Fort Hayes State University Kansas study

Personal Characteristics of successful Leaders

Successful leaders possess many characteristics. Some of these that especially appeal to me are:

Attitude

> "Attitude, not aptitude, determines your altitude."
>
> Zig Ziglar

> "If you think you can, or if you think you can't, you are right."
>
> Henry Ford

Have you ever come across a successful leader with a bad attitude? A negative, dispirited, can't be done attitude? No? I didn't think so! Successful leaders are invariably optimistic. Even when things are not going well, they always look on the bright side. We will prevail – we will succeed – we will win, is their mantra. Optimism has a hugely motivating effect on employees while, understandably, negativity has the opposite effect. As an example of optimism in really tough times, just read a few lines of one of Winston Churchill's famous speeches to the British public during the Second World War:

"We shall fight on the beaches, we shall fight on the landing grounds, we shall fight in the fields and in the streets, we shall fight in the hills; we shall never surrender,"

Passion

"Passion is the fire, the desire, the strength of conviction, and the drive that sustains the discipline to achieve your vision."

Dr. Stephen Covey

As a motor car can't move without fuel, a leader can't lead without passion. Passion is what drives leaders to achieve their goals and ultimately propels them ever closer to their respective visions. Passion is what inspires their followers to work harder, faster, longer, for common exciting goals. A disinterested, insipid, person lacking in any passion for the task in hand may occupy a leadership position, but will never rouse their people to high performance. We can't make others passionate about their life or work if we don't feel passionate about ours. Our followers get their energy directly from our personal passion and commitment. So, be passionate or be nothing!

Enthusiasm

"People, who never get carried away, should be."

Malcolm Forbes

"You will be fired with enthusiasm, or you will be fired, with enthusiasm."

Vince Lombardi

When I visited Green Bay in Wisconsin in October 2003, as part of my itinerary while serving as the International President of Toastmasters, I had the great honour of visiting the Green Bay Packers HQ. There I was escorted to Vince Lombardi's office and sat for a while in his personal armchair and reflected on his illustrious career in American Football. In 1958 when he took over as the general manager of the Green Bay Packers they had no clout in professional football, for they had won only one game the previous year. Under his leadership the same group of players improved dramatically and at Lambeau Field in Green Bay on December 31, 1961, Vince watched proudly as the Packers defeated the New York Giants 37-0 for the National Football League championship. Enthusiasm was an important ingredient in his personal makeup and he would not settle for less in his players. You will note the difference a single comma makes to the meaning of his words above. By the way, while there, I was very fortunate to receive as a gift a football signed by the great Brett Favre, a legend in American football circles!

Discipline

"Decide what it is you want to achieve.
Decide you're willing to pay the price to achieve it.
Pay the price."

Bunker Hunt, American oil billionaire's
recipe for success

Any worthwhile achievement requires effort, usually lots of effort over a period of time. No matter how brilliant your thoughts and ideas are, it takes discipline to turn them into reality. And this is what successful leaders do – driven on by their passion and enthusiasm for the task in hand, they persevere until the job is finished. My favorite example of incredible discipline is the story of Canadian Terry Fox. Terry was an active teenager involved in many sports. He was only 18 years old when he was diagnosed with bone cancer and forced to have his right leg amputated 15 centimeters (six inches) above the knee in 1977. While in hospital, Terry was so overcome by the suffering of other cancer patients, many of them young children, that he decided to run across Canada to raise money for cancer research.

He would call his journey the *Marathon of Hope.*

After 18 months and running over 5,000 kilometers (3,107 miles) to prepare, Terry started his run in St. John's, Newfoundland on April 12, 1980. He ran 42 kilometers (26 miles) a day through Canada's Atlantic Provinces, Quebec and Ontario.

However, on September 1st, after 143 days (he had one rest day) and 5,373 kilometers (3,339 miles), Terry was forced to stop running outside of Thunder Bay, Ontario, because cancer had appeared in his lungs. An entire nation was saddened. Terry passed away on June 28, 1981 at age 22. What an example of tremendous discipline and application. As a leader, it's fairly certain you will never be required to run the equivalent of a full marathon every day for 142 days, on one good leg .But there will be times when everything looks like too much hard work, when the struggle seems to be all uphill, when all the fates are conspiring against you. These are the times when real leaders step up to the plate, rally the troops by being optimistic about a successful outcome and never, ever think of throwing in the towel.

Getting your people
on the bus

Create an inspiring vision

As outlined earlier in the book, every successful leader has a vision of a desired future state. You must have some end result in mind or else you have little chance of achieving it. You are like a bus driver who doesn't know what his destination is supposed to be. So, he never leaves the bus garage. You will recall the advice Alice received from the Cheshire Cat when she asked him for directions – "If you don't know where you are going, any road will take you there". As the driver of your team's bus, if you don't know where your destination is, it's very unlikely that your bus will get anywhere either. So, your very first task as a leader is to have a clear destination in mind. We call it having a vision.

A Definition:

> "Vision is seeing with the mind's eye what is possible in people, in projects, in causes and in enterprises."
>
> Dr. Stephen Covey

What is a Vision Statement?

A Vision Statement is a short, succinct, and inspiring statement of what the organization intends to become and to achieve at some point in the future. It has been described as a compelling picture of the achievable, highly desired future. It describes aspirations for the future, although expressed in the present tense, without specifying the means that will be used to achieve those desired ends. The most effective visions are those that inspire, usually asking employees for the best, the most, or the greatest. Great leaders inspire great performance by creating in people's minds vivid images of where they are headed. This demands from leaders the ability to communicate this through constant repetition delivered with passion and conviction. This is also something that cannot be achieved overnight – it can take months, even years of effort. The sad thing is that so many "leaders" do not put in the necessary effort over time, or, indeed, any effort, to achieve this and then wonder why their people do not buy into it. As you can readily see from the following quote of Frances Burnett's, a new vision has to go through several stages of comprehension before finally being accepted.

> "At first people refuse to believe that a strange new thing can be done, then they hope it can be done, then they see it can be done — then it is done and the entire world wonders why it was not done centuries before"
> Frances Hodgson Burnett, 19th century
> American writer

The Vision Statement of Toastmasters International is an excellent example of a vision statement that is succinct, inspirational, and expressed as if it is already achieved.

> "Toastmasters International empowers people to achieve their full potential and realize their dreams. Through our member clubs, people throughout the world can improve their communication and leadership skills and find the courage to change."

Crafting a Vision Statement

These are some of the questions you must answer when crafting a vision statement.

- What does our organisation do well?

- What is the most important thing we want to do?

- What makes our organisation unique or special?

- What do we expect from our organisation?

- What makes us feel good about our organisation?

You will note from the Beacon Hospital example that its staff are given a key role in its vision, recognising that the desired standard of patient care cannot be delivered without them. How often do we see vision statements that make no mention of the very people without whom no success is possible.

"Our vision is to be a beacon of excellence in Irish healthcare. We will position ourselves as the predominant healthcare provider within the community we serve. Our services will be provided by dedicated, competent and talented people focused on continuous improvement and service excellence."

The Beacon Hospital, Sandyford, Co Dublin

Create a Mission Statement

A Mission Statement is a simple statement of what an organization does and should also describe the business the organization is in. It is a definition of "why" the organization currently exists. Each member of an organisation should be able to verbally express this mission

> We will provide exceptional patient care in an environment where quality, respect, caring and compassion are at the centre of all we do.
>
> The Beacon Hospital, Sandyford, Co Dublin

> Companies whose employees understand the mission and goals enjoy a 29 percent greater return than other firms
>
> Watson Wyatt Work Study

> U.S. workers want their work to make a difference, but 75% do not think their company's mission statement has become the way they do business
>
> Workplace 2000 Employee Insight Survey

These statistics make very interesting reading. How many companies have a mission and goals that their employees understand? Are these expressed in such a way that excites and motivates them? Is the mission statement totally different than the manner in which the companies operate? How would your company fare in such a survey?

Do the people who work for you know that there is such a thing as an organisation mission statement?

What are Values/Core Values

Values are fundamental beliefs held by an individual or organisation. Organisational core values represent frameworks for the way organisations do things. More and more studies show that successful companies place a great deal of emphasis on their values, which then underpin their vision. These values provide a framework for achieving the vision and increasing the effectiveness of the organisation. Values are at the very heart of corporate culture because they set out the dos and, by exception, the don'ts, of an organisation. For maximum effectiveness, values must be shared within the organisation (everyone must know and believe in them), and at all times lived up to. Because they permeate the entire organisation, people inside and outside the organisation can observe them, while every action taken is guided by them. Decisions are made with these values in mind and organisations accept and live with the results of their actions.

Three or four core values are usually sufficient. They usually refer to values such as integrity, honesty, fairness, respect, commitment, excellence, customer focus etc

The core values of Toastmasters International are, for example:
- Integrity

- Dedication to excellence

- Service to the member

- Respect for the individual

This is how the organization describes what these values mean to it. "These are values worthy of a great organization, and we believe we should incorporate them as anchor points in every decision we make. Our core values provide us with a means of not only guiding but also evaluating our operations, our planning and our vision for the future."

Decide your priorities

"Concentration — that is, the courage to impose on time and events his own decision as to what really matters and comes first — is the executive's only hope of becoming the master of time and events."

Peter Drucker, the Effective Executive

- Urgent and Important

There is never any argument about this priority. We all respond quickly to a problem which is urgent and important. If your house goes on fire, you are hardly likely to continue reading this book, for example. You will, no doubt, rush from the house immediately and call the fire brigade. If you get a sudden severe pain in your chest, you are not likely to go jogging or decide it's just the day to go mountain climbing. No, you will, as fast as you possibly can, attend the nearest doctor or hospital.

- Urgent and Not Important

Urgent and not important matters are invariably other people's problems who seek help and/or solutions from you. In other words, matters that are not important to you, have, for someone else, become urgent and important and now they have become urgent for you. As your boss is due to leave for a meeting, for example, he suddenly finds he is missing some important information. Your phone rings and now you have an urgent problem- even if it's not very important to you personally.

- Not Urgent and Not Important

Ah, the trivial items that we all just love spending our time attending to. We spend our time at these because, usually, they are relatively easy to do, give immediate feedback, and, most importantly, give us an excuse not to even think about the next category of priority! When we're busy we feel less guilty about not tackling the really important.

- Important but Not Urgent

All of us have great difficulty in finding time to attend to important but not urgent items. Mañana or tomorrow rules the day. Your health check up, that training course to update your skills, the new strategic plan for your department, can all be postponed or, as the saying goes, put on the long finger, for attention later. But, this is the temptation you must try to avoid at all costs. Because, if you do nothing about them, sooner or later, they will one day become both urgent and important. Is that the sound of an ambulance you hear? The time to attend to important things must be set aside at the expense of "not urgent and not important" and "urgent and not important".

Apply this rule to your business or job position. What are the most important challenges facing you? Prioritise these and then move on to the next step in being a successful leader.

> "Don't say you don't have enough time. You have exactly the same number of hours per day that were given to Helen Keller, Pasteur, Michelangelo, Mother Teresa, Leonardo de Vinci, Thomas Jefferson, and Albert Einstein."
>
> H. Jackson Brown

Build your team

> "Not finance. Not strategy. Not technology. It is teamwork that remains the ultimate competitive advantage, both because it is so powerful and so rare."
>
> Patrick Lencioni, author of "Five Dysfunctions of a Team"

> "A team is a small number of people with complimentary skills who are committed to a common purpose, set of performance goals and approach, for which they hold themselves mutually accountable"
>
> Jon R. Katzenbach and Douglas K. Smith, "The Discipline of Teams" Harvard Business Review, March- April 1993

A team is a group of people who work together to accomplish specific, common goals.

They share responsibility for their tasks and depend upon one another to achieve them.

Organising your team

- Begin with identifying the right mix of members

- Have a clear set of objectives which are spelled out as clearly as possible

- Establish parameters and controls

- Develop a plan

- Assign roles and responsibilities

- Establish metrics allowing team members to assess their performance and how this impacts on overall organisation performance

Never forget that teams that fail usually do so because they lack a clear purpose.

"One of the best indicators of the strength of a team is the "We to Me" ratio. How often do team members and leaders use "we" and "ours" instead of "I", "me" and "mine" in their conversations? "

Jim Clemmer, "The Leadership Digest"

Team leaders

They communicate well the organisation's vision, mission, and goals, while building team trust and encouraging participation from all involved. They make it easy for team members communicate with each other and with the team leader. They promote an open culture with ready access to management. Problem solving is facilitated by allowing input from everyone who can assist in finding a solution. They are always ready and eager to help team members grow and develop through ongoing training in communication, leadership, and other group skills. The leading world wide organisation in teaching communication and leadership skills is Toastmasters International with some 250,000 members, in 12,000 clubs, in 90 countries around the world. For further information go to www.toastmasters.org

"If you could get all the people in an organization rowing in the same direction, you could dominate any industry, in any market, against any competition, at any time".

Patrick Lencioni, author of "Five
Dysfunctions of a Team"

Team members must know

What they are supposed to do

It may sound strange but many cases of perceived under performance can be traced back to a lack of clear definition about what, exactly, is required to be done. Give hazy, unclear, or instructions capable of being misunderstood, and then don't be surprised when you do not get what you were expecting. The answer is to give your staff accurate job descriptions and then later ask them to tell you what they are supposed to do, in order to check their understanding. If it is a specific project, large or small, that needs to be done, then you should be very clear about what you are looking for as the desired outcome.

Why they are supposed to do it

The further down the ranks in any organisation people are, the less likely they are to know why their role is important. Basic knowledge of what the benefits to the organisation are for doing a job right, as well as the negative impact for doing it incorrectly, is the minimum every employee should know. So, it is necessary to describe the relationships between the different tasks employees perform, and how these relate to tasks and goals in other departments, to customers, and to the mission of the organisation.

> "Good leaders make people feel that they're at the very heart of things, not at the periphery. Everyone feels that he or she makes a difference to the success of the

organization. When that happens people feel centered and that gives their work meaning."

Warren Bennis

How they are supposed to do it

People may know what they are supposed to do and why it is important to do it, but not know how to do it. Sometimes it is mistakenly assumed that telling people to do something is teaching them. Telling people and even demonstrating is never enough. Actual practice, simulating, or doing the task, is the best way for people to learn. How will you know that they know how to do the task(s)? Simply ask them to describe it to you or have them demonstrate it.

How well they are expected to do it

To perform any task well employees must know the standard of performance that is expected of them. These standards could be quality based, quantity based, or timed based, or indeed all of these or any combination of them. It is the leader's job to ensure that these measurements or standards are known to all concerned.

How well they are doing

While the old adage what gets measured gets done is familiar to most of us, I have created a new maxim to go along with it which says, 'If I know how well I am doing, I will be motivated to work even harder' How do you let you staff know how well, or otherwise, they are doing? Have you systems in place to identify this and to communicate this to them?

"Individual commitment to a group effort — that is what makes a team work, a company work, a society work, a civilization work."

Vince Lombardi

A Smart Goal is:

S = Specific. It clearly states what must happen

M = Measurable. Results can be easily validated

A = Action-oriented. It begins with the word "to" followed by a verb

R = Realistic. It is challenging, yet practical and achievable

T = Time-bounded. It contains a timetable for achievement

An example would be "To complete writing my book on leadership by the 31st December this year"

The Implementation Process

Once goals have been determined, the planning process can be broken down into five easy steps:

1. Make a list of tasks according to their priority

2. Assign responsibilities to team members according to their suitability for the task.

3. Establish specific deadlines for their completion.

4. Monitor progress

5. Review regularly

The sequence can be expressed as plan, organise, monitor, and review. As time passes, and you review progress with your team, modify the plan as necessary. Challenges, and/or problems, will occur in every venture. Leaders must be flexible and be open and ready to change plans as required. The temptation always when things are working well is to neglect to carry out the review process. This is just as important to do in areas where there seems to be no problems as in areas where problems clearly exist.

Why is a plan important?

A plan describes how a goal will be achieved. It outlines the necessary activities, the resources to be allocated, who will be responsible for achieving it, and a time frame for completion. It gives direction to everyone involved in achieving the goal and ensures it will be achieved in as an efficient manner possible.

Planning is important for several reasons.

-   Planning forces leaders to identify the desired final outcome. When this is decided, they then go on to plan the steps necessary to achieve it.

-   Planning enables decisions to be coordinated, which eliminates or diminishes the possibility of conflict.

-   An action plan focuses everyone's mind on the important goals and how quickly and successfully they are being achieved.

-   Planning ensures efficient use of resources.

"Planning is bringing the future into the present so that you can do some thing about it now"

Alan Lakein

"He who fails to plan, plans to fail"

Anon

"A good plan today is better than a perfect plan tomorrow"

Alan Lakein

The importance of buy-in

You can have all the visions, missions, core values and objectives you like, but unless the people on your team buy in to them, you will not be successful. So what is the best way to achieve this vitally important buy-in? Well, let them know you need their support. Then give them an opportunity to have an imput into deciding, with you, what the team's goals and objectives should be. Familiarise them with your organisation's vision, mission and values. What almost always happens is that they thoroughly enjoy providing the input with their peers, feel involved with the process, realize the importance of their contributions, and feel they have a stake in the outcome. One of the extra bonuses arising from this involvement is that other problems, which may have remained hidden or dormant, will be identified and can be addressed through training or otherwise. All sorts of organizational and performance issues come to light and can be readily solved in this way. Common employee problems, from increased absenteeism and high turnover rates, to other issues such as low morale and performance will also be positively affected. The bottom line is, however, that unless you have credibility with your team and, most importantly of all, that they trust you, you will have an uphill battle on your hands. And don't be disappointed if you find that not everyone will buy in to your vision. Then it will be necessary for you to help them find some other position outside your team. In no circumstances can you allow them on your bus, as they will not be fully committed to your vision, objectives, and goals.

"When you need to move an organisation in a new direction, the staff will respond as follows. One third will say we always thought this new direction was a good idea. Another third can be persuaded by reasoned argument to accept the change. The final third you will have to remove from the bus"

Gerard Kleisterlee, President and
CEO, Royal Phillips Electronics, The
Netherlands

Keeping your people on the bus

You now have a vision, mission and plan in place. Your priorities are decided. You have assembled your team and got their buy-in by dint of your persuasive and inspirational communication skills. Everyone is in the right seat in the bus and because of your strong personal values, your team members completely trust you as their leader and are ready to move heaven and earth to achieve their (your!) goals. Now the bus, with you at the wheel, and all your team on board, takes to the road towards your final destination. Everybody is happy. What could possibly go wrong and prevent you from getting there. Well, your job is only half done, if even that. As you drive your bus ever onwards towards its destination, members of your team may get bored, dissatisfied, fed up and leave the bus, unless you take positive measures to keep them there. In real life, of course, members of teams do not usually physically leave, although this does happen. If people actually quit, you can always replace them, but at a cost, of course. What is far more insidious is when they switch off mentally and just go through the motions, or worse still work in a negative way at hampering progress. Your job as their leader is to ensure that neither of these events happens and this section of the book explains how you can achieve this.

Keep them in the picture

Your team will work a lot better when you keep them informed. Knowing the big picture and where they fit in is always very motivational. The opposite is also very true – team members who are not kept in the picture can be become demotivated and their work performance may suffer. The bigger the organization the bigger the challenge this becomes. The bigger your span of control is as a leader, the more it is necessary for you to keep this at the forefront of your communications with your team at all times. There is nothing worse than hearing employees moaning that nobody tells them anything. In the absence of factual information the vacuum is usually filled with rumor and misinformation. Morale is affected, focus wavers, and output is adversely affected.

Support your team

We all need support in one way or another. As the English poet, John Donne, once wrote, "No man is an island entire unto himself". We rely on other people to help us to get things done or to overcome various life challenges. We can get this support from parents, family, and friends in our private lives. At work we can get it from the organization, our boss, and our work colleagues. But now you are the boss. Do you readily support the members of your team? There are numerous examples of situations where this support is necessary and welcome. Here are some of them:

Overwork
Is this self inflicted or are staff members required to work long hours over an extended period. Nobody can work long hours for too long without something suffering e.g. quality of work, personal relationships inside and outside work, or health. Even if it is self inflicted, you still have a responsibility to do something about it.

Stress

What is causing this stress? Your job is to find to find out and deal with it. Heavens forbid it can be related directly to your leadership style.

Lack of clarity

This is totally the responsibility of the leadership team. It is the responsibility of this team to ensure that people understand their role, their duties, and how they fit in to the organisations "big picture".

Deadlines

Who sets these deadlines? Deadlines are necessary in getting things done but are there too many of them? Are they too demanding? Are they imposed or agreed?

Personal problems

Are there sympathetic processes and procedures in place to deal with personal problems when they inevitably arise?

Conflict

There is a special section later in this book dealing with this subject

Resources

Has your staff the necessary resources to do their jobs efficiently and effectively? Your staff will appreciate your support in this area more than most.

When team members feel they are supported by their leader, they will function much more effectively. They do not worry that they will be left to their own devices if problems arise. Many managers, who are not leaders, simply disappear when such problems appear and decisions are called for, leaving their employees to sort things out alone. If this is a consistent feature of the boss's behavior, it will impact very negatively on team performance.

Facilitate their work

The term facilitation is broadly used to describe any activity which makes easy the tasks of others. Teams can consist of very few, very many, or somewhere in between, number of members. The task of the leader, whatever the size of the team, is to ensure that they work together to achieve their goals. This is achieved by keeping in touch with progress, making any slight adjustments as necessary, keeping the team informed and sorting out any conflicts of time, resources, or personalities. The leader's role is to remove all obstacles to the success of the team, thus allowing them to focus completely on the desired outcomes.

Listen to them

"I don't want yes-men around me. I want everyone to tell the truth, even if it costs them their jobs"
Samuel Goldwyn

"None of us is as smart as all of us"
Japanese proverb

Of all the things a successful leader can afford not to do, is finding time to listen to their team members. Making himself/herself reasonably physically available to meet them when they need to talk or discuss matters of concern is obviously the first requirement. Absent, or unavailable, so called leaders do not lead for very long! Even when both sides do meet, team members will very quickly work out if their leader is only pretending to listen to them. The obvious signs are fiddling with phones, blackberries etc, or shuffling papers while they are speaking. Interrupting them while they are still speaking is another. At meetings, not asking all attendees their opinion sends its own very clear message that their views are not important. Even if their views are necessarily not adopted, people will, at least, if they are asked for their opinion, feel that their views were considered. Keep in mind that no one of us is as smart as all of us. If team members begin to believe that their leader is uninterested in listening them, then they stop offering opinions. This, surely, is more of a loss to the leader than the follower.

Give direction when required

In every organization, no matter how clear its plans and goals are, there will be occasions when team members will look for direction from their leader. This could be clarifying some matter, resolving priorities, or just looking for some advice. Conflicts in priorities do arise from time to time even in the best regulated circles and it is then that the leader is expected to give clear direction to enable the team to move on towards the goal. Not being available, or evading the issue, or refusing to make a decision when required, has the worst possible effect on individual and team morale.

Coach them

A definition of coaching can be expressed as the art of inspiring, energising and facilitating the performance, learning and development of the person being coached.

> "Coaching is a process that enables learning and development to occur and thus performance to improve"
> Eric Parsloe, "The Manager as Coach and Mentor" (1999)

Golf pros have coaches, football teams have coaches, opera singers even have coaches. Obviously coaches are regarded as must haves in these areas. So, do you take time to coach the people who report to you? What? Where would I get the time to do this, you cry? Well, if you are convinced that coaching is a critical leadership responsibility, you will organize your time accordingly. Coaching people effectively sets leaders apart from managers, most of whom are totally focused on bottom line performance and nothing else. Remember that you manage things but you lead people. Even if you make an appointment to spend one hour each week coaching a member of you staff, that is a start. Useful topics for discussion could be building on the strengths and working on eliminating the weaknesses of the staff members concerned. Another fruitful area always is discussing roles, responsibilities, and expectations. And your staff will have one more reason for staying on your bus.

Delegate and empower them

Delegation is, in all probability, the least understood, and most often mismanaged, aspect of leadership that I have experienced. More often than not it simply consists of an instruction to somebody to do some thing, with no other elaboration. Then there is total surprise and a gnashing of teeth when the desired outcome fails to materialize. You know when you are not delegating and empowering properly when team motivation is low, your team is looking confused and conflicts break out over small things. But the biggest sign that you are not delegating as well as you could be, is when you are being constantly asked questions about what you considered already delegated tasks. Worst still is when you end up actually doing them!

So what is delegation?

Delegation is the process of transferring the responsibility for a specific task to another person and _empowering_ that individual to accomplish the task effectively.

So what are the steps needed for effective delegation?

Beforehand

Select the person who will perform the task and having assessed the person's ability and readiness to do the task, decide if any training is necessary.

When you are delegating

Begin by explaining why completing the specific task is important. People will perform better when they clearly understand where the task fits into the "big picture". When they understand the "why", their performance is maximised.

Next agree the task and what you require as the desired specific outcome. But there is something else which is often overlooked and without which the task won't be completed satisfactorily. Without the necessary resources being made available, the job won't get done to anyone's satisfaction. Resources can include finance or assistance in different ways, or, what I consider to be even more important, the time to properly complete the task. Too often, people, who are already overburdened with work, have this extra task imposed on them, without any regard to whether they have the time to do it or not. Having satisfied yourself that all the necessary resources are available to both parties satisfaction, the final part of a properly delegated task is to agree deadlines for progress reports and the final completion date, while empowering the person to make decisions and act within agreed limits. Delegation and empowerment go hand in hand – delegation without empowerment won't work. But, unfortunately, you will have to, because, in its absence, you will be asked to make all the decisions.

Afterwards

Communicate as necessary, ensuring the person knows they have your full support while receiving and giving regular feedback on progress and results.

Levels of empowerment can be classified as follows.

Level 1.   Wait until told what to do

Level 2.   Ask for instructions and then carry them out

Level 3.   Bring recommendations and let the boss decide which one will be selected for action

Level 4.   Do it and report immediately

Level 5.   Do it and report routinely

Level 6.   Just do it

On what level do your reports operate? Wouldn't be great if they were all on level 5 or 6?

If empowerment is the key to delegation, what are the reasons why it happens so rarely? The first and principal reason is that managers do not wish to relinquish any control, either out of fear, or the need to micromanage everything. Another reason can be that the manager lacks the requisite delegation skills or, indeed, the employee lacks the skills to do the task. Sometimes, of course, employees just don't want the responsibility. Properly delegating to and empowering people takes time. That's something busy managers have in very short supply, precisely because they do not delegate and empower effectively. It truly is a vicious circle.

Give frequent feedback on performance

Feedback in a work setting can be defined as information given to one or more team members concerning their behaviour, attitude, relationships, and progress toward the achievement or non-achievement of objectives or goals

We all like to hear someone tell us when we are doing a good job. In fact, where we do not get such feedback we often can get resentful and our performance can suffer. How long does it take to tell someone that we appreciate what they are doing? It takes only seconds and yet how rare it is. Many years ago, I remember going to my boss and asked him to thank a colleague of mine who had worked very hard all that day without a break dealing with a serious crisis. He refused point blank, uttering the immortal words "Isn't that what he's getting paid for". However, there are also times when feedback is required to improve some facet of the person's performance. There are a number of important factors to keep in mind when you do this. Always do it in private, speaking for yourself and nobody else. Emphasise how the person's actions/inactions are affecting the team. Be specific in pointing out the area(s) where improvement is required, while acknowledging any good aspects of performance in other areas. Always end on a positive note. So it's a bit like a sandwich. Begin with some comment on any positive aspects of performance, in the middle mention the area where improvement is required, while ending once again in a positive way.

"Praise loudly, blame softly".

Catherine the Great

Develop them

"I have never found an organization in the world that over trains its people."

Charles Garfield, peak performance researcher and author

High performing organizations consistently invest from 3 - 5 percent of their payroll expenses in training.

Many lesser performing companies fall well below that. Many companies are so engrossed in everyday operational activities focused on bottom line performance that they fail to invest in developing their staff in order to ensure future growth and profits. Naturally, staff who feel their manager/company has an interest in developing their skills have a much greater interest in continuing to work for that manager/company. Their commitment is usually greater and they stay longer. A win/win outcome for each side.

Resolve conflict quickly

There is no workplace on earth where some conflict either great or small doesn't arise from time to time. To suggest otherwise is ignoring reality. But, in all cases, this isn't necessarily a bad thing, strange as it seems. As long as it is resolved effectively, it can have a very positive effect on performance. However, if conflict is not resolved effectively, it can lead to teamwork breaking down and personal issues becoming the everyday focus, rather than the appropriate goals.

In the 1970s, Kenneth Thomas and Ralph Kilman identified five main styles of dealing with conflict (Thomas-Kilman Conflict Mode Instrument) that vary in their degrees of cooperativeness and assertiveness. They argued that people typically have a preferred conflict resolution style. However, they also noted that different styles were most useful in different situations and each had its strengths and weaknesses.

Ignoring/Avoiding it:
In some situations the issue may not be important and it may be best to ignore it. Often though, it doesn't go away but festers.

Accommodating/Smoothing it over:
This method is appropriate when the issues are more important to the parties involved than they are to you and the team's goals. It preserves harmony.

Competitive/Forcing
A leader uses power to resolve differences. However, it usually results in "winners" and "losers" and losers can be resentful.

Compromising:

Each party makes a major concession to arrive at a solution. Since both parties lose something, they may have less support for the solution, however.

Collaborating

This is a good way to resolve conflict. Each side recognises the other's needs as legitimate and important while acknowledging each other's ability and experience. When they work together to arrive at an agreement that will resolve the conflict each party feels they win so that they are more committed to the outcome.

Recognise and appreciate them and then recognise and appreciate them some more!

"Motivate them, train them, care about them, and make winners of them"

J.W. Marriott Chairman Marriot Hotels

"Money won't make you happy, but happy people will make you money"

The Financial Times, London

"The deepest craving in human beings is the need to be appreciated"

Psychologist William James

People respond positively to positive behavior. So you need to constantly recognize achievement when it's due. Tell the team about an individual's success. Celebrate all successes both team and individual. Specifically, a leader gives praise and positive recognition while using ritual and ceremony. One of the golden rules is to always give your team credit for your achievements and successes and resist the temptation to keep it for yourself. In any event most times it is your team that is responsible anyway.

> "The important thing to recognize is that it takes a team, and the team ought to get credit for the wins and the losses. Successes have many fathers, failures have none."
>
> Philip Caldwell

See also "Giving frequent feedback on performance"

Would I follow me?

> "After 20 years of research and 60,000 exit interviews, the Saratoga Institute reports that 80% of turnover is related to unsatisfactory relationships with the boss. Talent retention and engagement will remain one of management's highest priorities over the coming years. Indeed, in the so-called new economy with its ever-increasing reliance on talent

and technology, retention and engagement are critical to an organization's survival."

Marcus Buckingham, author of "First Break All the Rules: What the World's Greatest Managers Do Differently" and "Now Discover Your Strengths"

This is a great question to ask yourself. For a minute or two put yourself in the place of the people whom you manage and lead and consider how they might regard you as their leader. Would they support you through thick and thin in any venture you are engaged in, or would they just pay lip service to the idea and feebly go through the motions? Have you asked yourself why so many people look for transfers (if they do) out of your department? Have you asked the people concerned? The evidence revealed in the Saratoga Institute's findings is pretty compelling, would you not agree? 80% of turnover of staff is related to unsatisfactory relationships with the boss. In other words, 4 of every 5 staff leave because of how they feel about their boss. They leave his/her bus, and all the time and money spent in recruiting, training and generally developing them, is more or less wasted. I think it can be fairly construed that the bosses in these cases were managers not leaders. They managed "things" but paid little or no heed to "people" and their wants, needs, and desires.

"People join companies but they leave managers"
Marcus Buckingham

The Leadership Bus | 71

Communicate effectively

Effective communication by leadership in three critical areas is the key to winning organisational trust and confidence.

Explaining the company's overall business strategy to each employee is an important first step. Next is helping employees understand how what they do contributes to achieving key business objectives. Finally, share with them how the company is doing and how the employees own department is doing relative to the business objectives and what the focus is right now.

According to a mammoth research study conducted by the Gallup Organisation involving some 80,000 managers across different industries, and published in "First Break all the Rules" by Marcus Buckingham, the people who work for you want you to be really clear.

- *Tell us who we are supposed to serve*

- *Tell it to us vividly*

- *Tell us what our strengths are*

- *What's our score?*

- *What actions are we going to take right now?*

And Finally.....

It is the case that some leaders appear as if they were born with these skills. But just as management skills can be learned, so, too, can leadership skills. Whatever the level of your particular leadership skills, they can be quickly enhanced by putting into practice the ideas covered in this book. The questions you need to keep asking yourself are:

- Have you a vision of what you want to achieve (in the bus analogy – your destination)

- Have you convinced everyone, whose assistance you need to achieve it, to join you in the endeavour (are all your people on your bus and in the right seats)

- Are you ensuring that every member of your team is totally focused on the desired outcome (keeping them on the bus)

Nobody becomes an outstanding leader overnight. It takes time, patience and a belief that people will respond better to an approach which involves them to the fullest in whatever business they're in. As Stephen Covey says there is only individual behaviour and everything else flows out of that. You, as somebody's (many people's) leader, are that individual.

"Followers expect four things from their leaders: honesty, competence, vision and inspiration."

Kouses and Posner "The Leadership Challenge"

To lead yourself, use your head. To lead others use your heart."

Anon

"In a very real sense there is no such thing as organisational behaviour. There is only individual behaviour. Everything else flows out of that"

Dr Stephen Covey

My personal plan

- The actions I plan to take after today are…

- These will help me in the following ways…

- This is important to me because…

- I plan to complete these actions by (date)…

- My reward for completion will be…

"I am always doing that which I can not do, in order that I may learn how to do it"

Pablo Picasso

Remember the elevator to success is out of service — but the stairs are always open"

Zig Ziglar

"Leaders are made, they are not born. They are made by hard effort, which is the price which all of us must pay to achieve any goal that is worthwhile".

Vince Lombardi

The last word

I'll leave the final words to the business author Brian Tracy.

"Your ability to negotiate, communicate, influence, and persuade others to do things is absolutely indispensable to everything you accomplish in life. The most effective men and women in every area are those who can quite competently organize the cooperation and assistance of other people toward the accomplishment of important goals and objectives".

Bibliography

The Leadership Challenge, 3rd Edition. James M. Kouzes, Barry Z. Posner, ISBN 0-7879-6833-1, August 2003, Jossey-Bass

The New Leaders, Daniel Goleman, Richard Boyatzis, Anne McKee, ISBN 0751533815, 2003, Time Warner

Working with Emotional Intelligence, Daniel Goleman, ISBN 0-553-84023-1, 1998, Bantam Books

The One Minute Manager meets the Monkey, Ken Blanchard, William Oncken Jr., Hal Burrows. 1st Edition, ISBN 0-688-10380-4, Wm Morrow and Co New York

Why employees don't do what they are supposed to do and what to do about it, Ferdinand F Fournies, ISBN 0071342559, April 1999, McGraw-Hill

First, Break All the Rules: What the World's Greatest Managers Do Differently, Marcus Buckingham, Curt Coffman, ISBN 0684852861, May 1999, Simon and Schuster

The 8th Habit: From Effectiveness to Greatness, Stephen R. Covey, ISBN 0684846659, November 2004, Free Press

The Effective Executive, Peter Drucker, ISBN-13 978-0887306129, April 1993, HarperCollins

The Five Dysfunctions of a Team, Patrick Lencioni, ISBN-13 978-0787960759, March 2002, Jossey-Boss,

The Leaders Digest: Timeless Principles for Team and Organisation Success, Jim Clemmer, ISBN-13 978-0968467510, March 2003, Clemmer Group Pr

The Manager as Coach and Mentor, Eric Parsloe, ISBN-13 978- 0852928035, Sept 1999 Chartered Institute of Personnel and Management; 2nd Edition

The 7 Habits of Highly Effective People, Stephen R Covey, ISBN-13 978-0743269513, Nov 2004, Free Press

Lightning Source UK Ltd.
Milton Keynes UK
20 May 2010

154444UK00001B/10/P